review

Trucks Can Do a Lot

By Liza Charlesworth

ISBN: 978-1-339-02685-5

Art Director: Tannaz Fassihi; Designer: Tanya Chernyak
Photos © Getty Images and Shutterstock.com.

3 4 5 6 7 8 9 10 68 32 31 30 29 28 27 26 25 24

Printed in Jiaxing, China. First printing, August 2023.

Honk, honk!
It is a man in a truck.
Trucks can do a lot.

A truck can dig up sand.

A truck can spin and mix.

A truck can tip its bed
and drop rocks in a pit.
Tip, dump, bump!

This truck is a big help.
It is red and has a pump.
It's quick and can zip to a fire!

This truck can help as well.
It picks up bags of trash
on the block.

Is this truck big? No!
But it can lift a big box
at the dock.

This truck cannot dig or mix.
It cannot spin, lift, or dump.
But it can make kids say, "YUM!"